Tornadoes

by Julie Murray

Dash!
LEVELED READERS

3

3 Dash!
LEVELED READERS

Level 1 – Beginning
Short and simple sentences with familiar words or patterns for children who are beginning to understand how letters and sounds go together.

Level 2 – Emerging
Longer words and sentences with more complex language patterns for readers who are practicing common words and letter sounds.

Level 3 – Transitional
More developed language and vocabulary for readers who are becoming more independent.

abdopublishing.com

Published by Abdo Zoom, a division of ABDO, P.O. Box 398166, Minneapolis, Minnesota 55439.
Copyright © 2018 by Abdo Consulting Group, Inc. International copyrights reserved in all countries.
No part of this book may be reproduced in any form without written permission from the publisher.

Printed in the United States of America, North Mankato, Minnesota.
092017
012018

Photo Credits: iStock, Shutterstock, ©USACE p. 16, ©NOAA p. 17
Production Contributors: Kenny Abdo, Jennie Forsberg, Grace Hansen, John Hansen
Design Contributors: Dorothy Toth

Publisher's Cataloging in Publication Data
Names: Murray, Julie, author.
Title: Tornadoes / by Julie Murray.
Description: Minneapolis, Minnesota: Abdo Zoom, 2018. | Series: Wild weather |
    Includes online resource and index.
Identifiers: LCCN 2017939264 | ISBN 9781532120909 (lib.bdg.) | ISBN 9781532122026 (ebook) |
    ISBN 9781532122583 (Read-to-Me ebook)
Subjects: LCSH: Tornadoes--Juvenile literature. | Weather--Juvenile literature. | Environment--Juvenile
    literature.
Classification: DDC 551.553--dc23
LC record available at https://lccn.loc.gov/2017939264

Table of Contents

Tornadoes

Tornadoes are powerful storms. They may not last long, but they can cause a lot of **damage**. Many people call them "twisters."

About 1,200 tornadoes touch down in the U.S. each year. The state of Texas has the most tornadoes. Roughly 125 hit there every year.

7

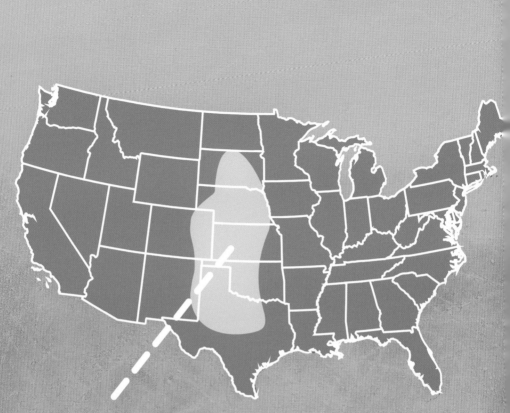

Tornado Alley

Most tornadoes occur in "tornado alley." This is an area of flat land between the Rocky Mountains and the Appalachian Mountains.

Tornadoes can hit other parts of the country too.

How They Form

Thunderstorms can form tornadoes. Large thunderstorms happen when warm and cold air meet.

The winds begin to spin in a circle forming a funnel cloud. It is named this because it is shaped like a funnel.

The funnel drops out of the storm clouds. If it hits the ground it is called a tornado. Tornadoes create a path of **destruction** as they move across the ground.

Tornadoes can have wind speeds up to 300 mph (482 kph).

This is strong enough to pick up cars and houses. Tornadoes are like huge vacuums. They can suck up anything in their path and tear it apart.

The average tornado lasts only 5 minutes and travels 7 miles (11 km). That was not the case in Joplin, Missouri, on May 22, 2011. That tornado was on the ground for 38 minutes. It covered 22 miles (35 km).

Stay Safe

Meteorologists track storms with radars, satellites, and **weather balloons**. These tools help them **predict** when and where a tornado will occur.

Many areas have tornado
sirens. These warn people
that a tornado is near.

Be sure to seek shelter in a basement or center of a house away from windows. Doing this could save your life!

- More tornadoes hit the U.S. than any other country.

- A waterspout is like a tornado over water. It can form over a lake, river, or ocean.

- A tornado is measured by its wind **damage**. EF0 is the weakest and EF5 is the strongest.

Glossary

damage – harm that makes something less useful or valuable.

destruction – the act of ruining completely.

meteorologist – a weather forecaster.

predict – say that a specified thing will happen in the future.

weather balloon – a balloon used to carry instruments into the sky to gather meteorological data in the atmosphere.

Index

Online Resources

Booklinks
NONFICTION NETWORK
FREE! ONLINE NONFICTION RESOURCES

To learn more about tornadoes, please visit **abdobooklinks.com**. These links are routinely monitored and updated to provide the most current information available.